Serenade in C, Op. 48

and

Suite No. 4, Op. 61
"Mozartiana"

in Full Score

Peter Ilyitch
TCHAIKOVSKY

DOVER PUBLICATIONS, INC.
Mineola, New York

Bibliographical Note

This Dover edition, first published in 1998, is a new compilation of two works originally published separately in early authoritative editions, n.d. Lists of instrumentation, notes to
"Mozartiana," and all English headings are newly added.

International Standard Book Number: 0-486-40414-5

Manufactured in the United States of America
Dover Publications, Inc., 31 East 2nd Street, Mineola, N.Y. 11501

CONTENTS

Serenade in C

for String Orchestra

Op. 48 (1880)

INSTRUMENTATION

Violins I, II [Violine]

Violas

Cellos [Violoncello]

Basses [Kontrabaß]

I. Piece in form of a sonatina

Andante non troppo *(tempo del comincio)*

sempre marcatissimo

II. Waltz

15

III. Elegy

IV. Finale
(Russian Theme)

Suite No. 4 in G
"Mozartiana"

Op. 61 (1887)

The suite consists of four movements based on the following works by Mozart:

    I. Gigue in G Major, K574 (1789)

    II. Minuet in D Major, K355/576b (ca. 1786)

    III. *Prayer* draws on Franz Liszt's organ transcription of Mozart's motet *Ave Verum Corpus*, K618 (1791).

    IV. Theme and Variations is derived from Mozart's *Variations on a Theme by Gluck*, K455 (1784) — itself based on the melody "Unser dummer Pöbel meint" from Gluck's operetta *La rencontre imprévue* (The Pilgrims of Mecca).

INSTRUMENTATION

2 Flutes [Flauti, Fl.]
2 Oboes [Oboi, Ob.]
2 Clarinets in A, B♭ ("B"), C [Clarinetti, Cl.]
2 Bassoons [Fagotti, Fg.]

4 Horns in F [Corni, Cor.]
2 Trumpets in B♭ ("B") [Trombe, Tbe.]

Timpani [Timp.]

Percussion
    Cymbals [Piatti]
    Glockenspiel (Bells*) [Jeu de Cloches, Cloch.]

Harp [Arpa]

Violins I, II [Violini, Vl.]
Violas [Viole, Vle.]
Cellos [Violoncelli, Vc.]
Basses [Contrabassi, Cb.]

*Theme and Variations, p. 59, lists *Jeu de Cloches* [tubular bells] as well as glockenspiel; however, Variation VIII, p. 79—the only time such an effect is called for—appears to be scored for glockenspiel alone.

I. Gigue

II. Minuet

Moderato

III. Prayer

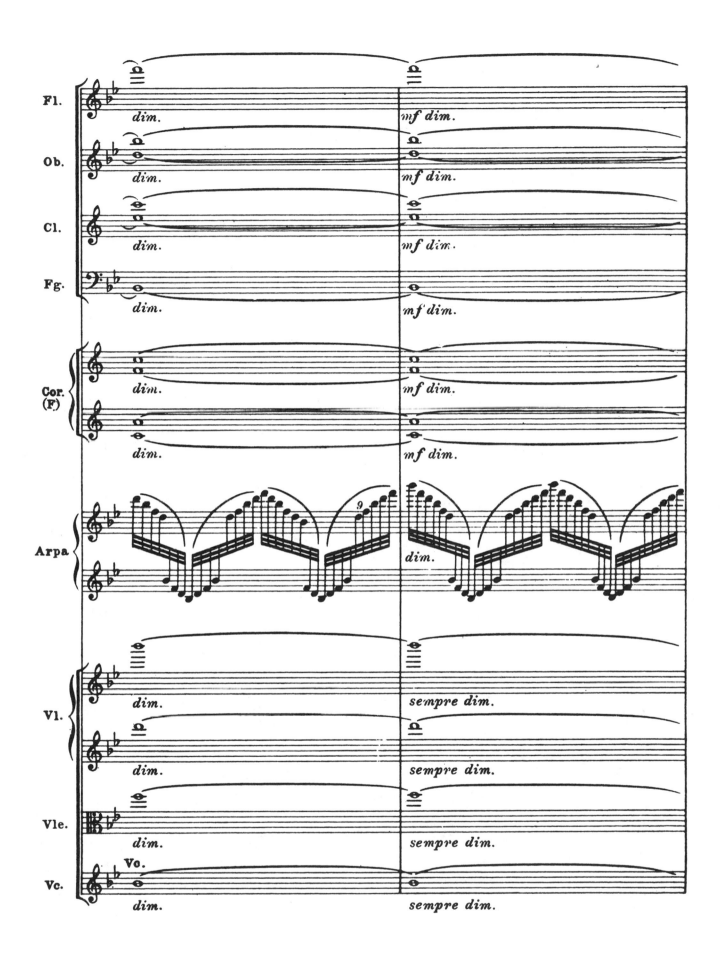

IV. Theme and Variations

Var. I

Var. II

Var. III

Var. IV

Var. VI

Var. VII

Var. VIII

Var. IX
Adagio

Var. X
Allegro vivo

END OF EDITION